Changes
A Bite to Eat

by Liz Gogerly

HODDER
Wayland

an imprint of Hodder Children's Books

Text copyright © 2002 Hodder Wayland

Project manager: Liz Gogerly
Designer: Peta Morey
Picture Research: Shelley Noronha at Glass Onion Pictures
Consultant: Norah Granger

Published in 2002 by Hodder Wayland, an imprint of
Hodder Children's Books

British Library Cataloguing in Publication Data
Gogerly, Liz
A bite to eat. - (Changes ; 3)
1. Food habits - Great Britain - History - 19th century - Juvenile literature
2. Food habits - Great Britain - History - 20th century - Juvenile literature
I.Title
394.1'0941'09034

ISBN 0 7502 3967 0

Printed and bound in
Italy by G. Canale & Co

Hodder Children's Books
A division of Hodder Headline Limited
338 Euston Road, London NW1 3BH

PICTURE ACKNOWLEDGEMENTS:
The publisher would like to thank the following for allowing their
pictures to be used in this publication:
Bridgeman 6 (top), 18 (top); Education Photos, John Walmsley 17 (bottom);
Mary Evans 5 (top and bottom), 14 (top); Angela Hampton 8 (bottom),
16 (bottom); Hulton Getty 4 (top), 9 (top), 11 (top), 12 (top), 17 (top), 19 (top);
Hodder Wayland Picture Library 14 (bottom), 15 (top); Impact 6 (bottom)/
Peter Arkell 7 (bottom); Billie Love (title page); Zul Mukhida 12 (bottom);
Museum of London 7 (top), 10 (top), !9 (bottom); National Portrait Gallery
8 (top); Yiorgos Nikiteas 10 (bottom); Photofusion/ Bob Watkins 4 (bottom);
Popperfoto 9 (bottom), 13 (top and bottom); Topham Picturepoint
15 (bottom); Hodder Wayland Picture Library (main cover); Photodisc (cover
inset).
With special thanks to Harvester for kind permission to use the
picture on page18 (bottom).

Contents

Time for Breakfast

Eating a proper breakfast is important for our **health**. Many people eat toast or cereals for breakfast. In the past people tried to eat the best breakfast they could afford. Poorer families mainly ate bread but hot foods such as **porridge** or eggs were also **popular**.

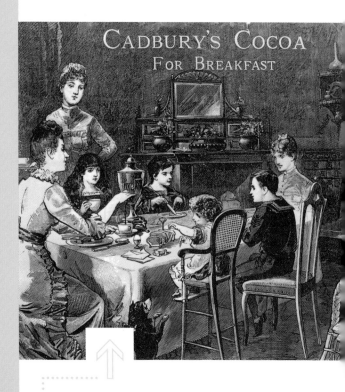

More well-off **Victorian** families had **kippers** or a rice dish called **kedgeree** for breakfast. This family has eggs with toast. They are drinking **cocoa** because it was **popular** for breakfast at that time.

This **advertisement** from about 1900 is for Shredded Wheat. People started eating cereals like these because they were easy to prepare and they did not need to be cooked.

This family from the 1960s is eating cereals and eggs for their breakfast. Now many families only eat breakfast together at the weekends. How often do you eat breakfast with your family?

Lunch Hour

In the past lunch was the main meal of the day for working people. Families often went home at lunchtime. This changed because people worked further away from their homes. Now most people eat lunch at work or school. Some people take a packed lunch or buy sandwiches.

In **Victorian** times most families thought it was important to eat lunch together on Sunday. This family is eating a pie. It would probably have been the best meal of the week. What kind of meals do you have on Sundays?

This **restaurant** in the 1960s provided **cheap**, hot and filling lunches. People could have soup, a **main course** and a pudding! Nowadays most people prefer lighter lunches such as sandwiches.

Free school meals were introduced for some children during the **Second World War**. The **government** thought it was important that every child had at least one good meal a day.

Dinner is Served

In the past families usually ate dinner together. It was the time when the whole family could talk about their day. These days parents and children often eat at different times. Children eat when they get in from school. Parents eat when they have finished work.

More well-off **Victorians** usually ate their main meal of the day in the evening. On special occasions they held large **dinner parties**. **Servants** would serve the food. What do you think the people in this picture might have eaten at dinner?

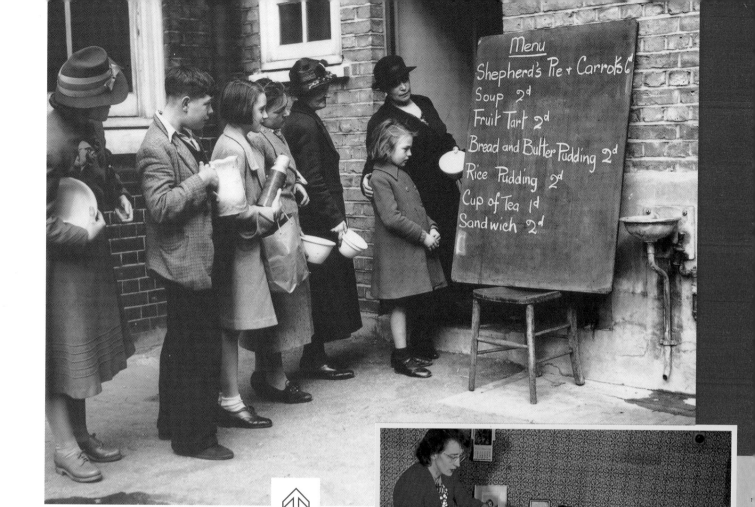

Menu
Shepherd's Pie + Carrots 6d
Soup 2d
Fruit Tart 2d
Bread and Butter Pudding 2d
Rice Pudding 2d
Cup of Tea 1d
Sandwich 2d

During the **Second World War** lots of homes were bombed. Many people had nowhere to cook so they collected their dinner from special **canteens**.

In the 1950s families usually ate their dinner together. There was not as much choice of food as we have today. All the family ate the same food. Everyone was expected to eat up every bit!

Between Meals

Many people eat snacks between meals. Some people like sweets or cakes. Other people prefer healthy treats like fruit or yoghurt. In the past sweets were usually only eaten at the weekend. Fruit was such a treat it was sometimes given as a Christmas present!

These **Victorian** children are **queuing** to buy ice-cream. Like today, street-sellers sold snacks such as hot potatoes or chestnuts, and sometimes cups of tea and coffee.

These people from the 1930s are enjoying afternoon tea. Cakes and sandwiches were served with pots of tea. This happened every day in richer people's homes.

These school children from 1949 are enjoying their bottles of milk. School children were given free milk every day until the 1970s. Can you guess why they were given free milk?

In the Kitchen

In **Victorian** times making food was hard work. Fires needed to be lit. All food had to be chopped and mixed by hand. Today we have **food-processors** and **microwave ovens.** Now making food can be quick, easy and fun!

In big **Victorian** houses there were large kitchens. There were usually cooks and **maids**. There were lots of kitchen **utensils** that were worked by hand. Can you name any of the **utensils** that are being used in this kitchen?

Even in the 1940s some people had to make a fire for cooking. This woman is making dinner on a **cast-iron range.** She would have boiled water for a bath here too.

These people from the 1950s are lucky because they have **fitted cupboards** and an electric fridge. This kind of kitchen would have been expensive in those days.

New Ways with Food

In our fridges and freezers we have lots of fresh things to eat and drink. People **store** cheese, eggs, salad and vegetables to eat. They keep orange juice and milk to drink. In the past people did not have fridges or freezers. They had to find other ways to store food.

HEINZ TOMATO SOUP.

In **Victorian** times **canned food** became **popular**. This family is enjoying tomato soup. For many people, **canned salmon** and **canned** peaches became a special treat on Sunday.

During the **Second World War** there was not enough food to eat in Britain. We needed to get food from **overseas**. **Canned** food like baked beans and milk could be brought across the sea and stored for a long time without **going off**.

Frozen food became available in Britain during the 1950s. At first frozen peas and **herrings** were **popular**. Then new foods like fish fingers and steak pies became favourites.

Shopping Around

In the past, people had to shop more often because they could not **store** food for long. They did not have supermarkets like we have now. They usually visited lots of smaller shops, like **bakeries** or **butchers**, that sold one kind of food.

This **Victorian** street-seller is selling fresh fruit and vegetables in the street. He walked from street to street calling out 'Fresh fruit! Fresh fruit!'. He would have walked many kilometres each day.

In the past people often had their food **delivered**. This photograph from 1938 shows a delivery boy for a confectioner's shop. It sold cakes, sweets and bread. Have you been to a shop like this?

These women from the 1980s are at a street market. They can buy **sweet potatoes** and **plantains**. These foods are used in **West Indian** cookery. You cannot always find these foods in a supermarket.

Eating Out

People in the past did not eat out like we do today. They would have been amazed at the choice we have. We can have a quick burger from a **fast-food restaurant**. We can have Sunday lunch at a **pub**. We can try foods from **overseas** at lots of different kinds of restaurant. We can even order a **take-away** pizza to eat at home.

In **Victorian** and **Edwardian** times many people liked to have afternoon tea at a **tea-room**. The children were expected to be well behaved. Have you ever been to a **tea-room**? What did you have to eat?

In the 1950s and 1960s many people moved to Britain from **overseas**. Italian, Chinese and Indian **restaurants** started to open. These women from the 1950s are trying Chinese food.

Fast food like burgers and hot-dogs were an American idea. In the 1960s **fast-food restaurants** started to become **popular** in Britain too. The food was **cheap** and could be eaten quickly.

Notes for Parents and Teachers

Changes and the National Curriculum

The books in this series have been chosen so that children can learn more about the way of life of people in the past. Titles such as *A Bite to Eat, Beside the Sea, Dressing Up, Home Sweet Home, School Days* and *Toys and Games* present children with subjects they already know about from their own experiences of life. As such these books may be enjoyed at home or in school, as they satisfy a number of requirements for the Programme of Study for history at Key Stage 1.

These books combine categories from 'Knowledge, skills and understanding' and 'Breadth of study' as required by the National Curriculum. In each spread, the photographs are presented in chronological order. The first photograph is a modern picture that the child should recognize. The following pictures are all historical. Where possible, a wide variety of pictures, including paintings, posters, artefacts and advertisements have been selected. In this way children can see the different ways in which the past is represented. A lively selection of pictures also helps to develop the children's skills of observation. In turn, this will encourage them to ask questions and discuss their own ideas.

The text is informative and raises questions for the children to talk about in class or at home. It is supported by further information about the historical photographs (see right). Once the children are familiar with the photographs you could ask them to guess when the pictures were taken – if it isn't mentioned in the text. By looking at clues such as clothes, hairstyles, style of buildings and vehicles they might be able to make reasonable guesses. There are further questions to ask your child or class on the right.

About the Photos

Time for Breakfast
Pages 4–5

An advertisement for Cadbury's Cocoa from 1886.
Question to ask:
- Do you ever drink cocoa at breakfast?

An advertisement for Shredded Wheat from about 1900.
Questions to ask:
- Do you think that cereals are good for you?
- Do you think that this advertisement is funny?

A family eating breakfast together in the 1960s.
Questions to ask:
- Do you ever sit down to breakfast with your family?
- How many cups can you see on the table?

Lunch Hour
Pages 6–7

A painting called *One of the Family* by Frederick George Cotman (1850–1920).
Questions to ask:
- What kind of pie do you think the family is eating?
- What do you think the people are drinking?

A restaurant called J. Lyons in the 1960s.
Questions to ask:
- Can you see some of the food people are eating?
- How can you tell these people have helped themselves to the food?

Lunchtime at a London school, *circa* 1990s.
Questions to ask:
- Do you think this food looks healthy to eat?
- What vegetables can you see?

Dinner is Served
Pages 8–9

A painting called *Dinner at Haddo House* from about 1884 by Alfred Emslie.

Questions to ask:
- Do you think this dinner party was a special occasion?
- Can you count how many people are sitting down?

Queuing at a makeshift canteen in September 1940.

Questions to ask:
- Do you like the food on the menu?
- What are the people holding and why?

A couple with seven children eating dinner in 1958.

Questions to ask:
- Can you see what the family has eaten for dinner?
- What do you think is in the bowl in the middle of the table?

Between Meals
Pages 10–11

Children queuing for half-penny ices in London, in 1876.

Questions to ask:
- Do you think it was a hot day?
- Do you still see people selling ice-creams this way?

Afternoon tea on the lawn in 1931.

Questions to ask:
- What kinds of cake are these people eating?
- Do you think they are having a good time?

Drinking milk at school in about 1949.

Questions to ask:
- Would you like to drink milk at school every day?
- Do you know why milk is good for your teeth and bones?

In the Kitchen
Pages 12–13

The kitchens at Royal Holloway College in Egham, Surrey, *circa* 1889–1893.

Question to ask:
- Have you ever visited a kitchen like this?

A Welsh miner's wife preparing an evening meal in 1941.

Questions to ask:
- What do you think the woman is cooking?
- How did people boil water for a cup of tea?

A couple in a modern kitchen in 1958.

Question to ask:
- What food can you see in this kitchen?

New Ways with Food
Pages 14–15

An advertisement for Heinz Tomato Soup from about 1900.

Questions to ask:
- Are you surprised that these people are eating tomato soup?
- Do you enjoy tomato soup?

A selection of tinned and powdered foods from the 1940s.

Questions to ask:
- Do you know any of the foods you can see here?
- Have you tasted tinned milk?

Shopping at the frozen food section in the 1950s.

Questions to ask:
- Which frozen foods can you see in this freezer?
- Do we have a bigger selection of frozen foods now?

Shopping Around
Pages 16–17

A street seller in London, *circa* 1877.

Questions to ask:
- This seller does not have very much to sell. What do you think he might have sold?
- Do you think he makes very much money from his job?

A confectionery and baker's shop in Bradford, *circa* 1938.

Question to ask:
- Do people get food delivered to their home these days?

At a London market, *circa* 1980s.

Questions to ask:
- What vegetables can you see at these stalls?
- Is there a street market where you live?

Eating Out
Pages 18–19

A painting called *Tea at Gunters* by John Strickland (1908–96)

Question to ask:
- How many maids can you see in this picture?

Two women try Chinese food at a recently opened Chinese restaurant in London in 1956.

Questions to ask:
- What are these women eating with?
- Can you name any of the foods they are eating?

A woman trying a 'bender' at a Wimpy burger restaurant in the 1950s.

Questions to ask:
- Can you see what this woman is eating?
- What kinds of fast food do you like?

Glossary

advertisement Words and pictures that are used to sell something to people.

bakeries Shops that sell fresh bread and cakes.

butchers Shops where meat is sold.

canned food Specially treated food that is put in tin cans and lasts for years.

canteens Areas at school or work where food can be eaten.

cast-iron range A stove that uses a fire to heat food.

cheap Describes something that does not cost much money.

cocoa A chocolate-tasting drink that is made with hot milk and cocoa powder.

delivered To have someting brought to you.

dinner parties Special dinners when family and friends are invited round to your home to eat.

Edwardian Used to describe anything or anybody from the time of King Edward VII (1901–1910).

fast food Food such as burgers and chips that can be prepared quickly.

fitted cupboards Specially designed furniture that can go in a kitchen.

food-processors Electrical machines with blades that can quickly slice or mix different kinds of food.

going off Turning bad.

government The people who are in charge of running a country.

health The strength and fitness of a person.

herrings A kind of fish.

kedgeree A rice dish made with fish and hard-boiled eggs.

kippers Herrings that have been smoked.

maids Women who are paid to do household jobs for somebody else.

main course Often the biggest and most filling dish at dinner.

microwave oven An electric oven that cooks by passing microwaves through the food.

overseas Other countries separated from your country by sea.

plantains Tropical fruits that look a bit like bananas.

popular Liked and enjoyed by a lot of people.

porridge A hot breakfast food that is made from oats and water or milk.

pub A place where meals and drinks are served. Pub is short for public house.

queuing Waiting in a line of people.

restaurant A place where people pay to eat meals.

salmon A kind of fish.

Second World War The world war that started in 1939 and ended in 1945.

servants People who do housework and other jobs for somebody else.

store To put things away until you need to use them.

sweet potatoes Tropical vegetables that are a kind of potato.

take-away A meal that you buy at a restaurant to eat somewhere else.

tea-room A place that serves tea, cakes and light meals.

utensils Tools that are used in the kitchen to help to prepare food. A hand-mixer is one kind of utensil.

Victorian Used to describe anything from the time of Queen Victoria (1837–1901).

West Indian Describes anything or anybody that comes from a place overseas called the West Indies.

Further Information

Books to Read
Non-fiction
History from Photographs: Food by Kath Cox (Hodder Children's Books, 1996)
Kitchens Through the Ages by Richard Wood (Hodder Wayland, 1997)
Why Should I Eat Well? by Claire Llewellyn and Mike Gordon (Hodder Wayland, 2000)

Fiction
Don't Forget the Bacon by Pat Hutchins (Red Fox, 2002)
I Will Not Ever Never Eat a Tomato by Lauren Child (Orchard, 2001)
Pumpkin Soup by Helen Cooper (Corgi, 1998)
The Very Hungry Caterpillar by Eric Carle (Hamish Hamilton Children's Books, 1995)

Sources
A History of Food: From Manna to Microwave by Margaret Leeming (BBC Books, 1995)
A Slice of Life: The British Way of Eating Since 1945 by Christina Hardyment (BBC Books, 1995)
Food In England by Dorothy Hartley (Little, Brown and Company, 1954)

Websites
http://www.gti.net/mocolib1/kid/food.html
A timeline for food which tells you when certain foods were introduced and when they became popular. Also suggests links to other sites where you can find more background information about different foods through the ages.

Websites for Teachers
http://www.educate.org.uk/teacher_zone/classroom/history/unit2.htm
Includes a lesson plan based around making the home corner into an old-fashioned kitchen.
http://www.primaryresources.co.uk/history/history.htm
Includes downloadable worksheets of a blank Second World War ration book, and a recipe for wartime fruitcake.
http://www.primaryresources.co.uk/harry/general4.htm
Includes many lively ways for teachers to use the Harry Potter books during lessons. Includes a blank menu on which children can come up with a menu for the 'Monster Cafe' that is featured in Hogsmeade.

Index